Level C · Book 3

QuickReads®
A Research-Based Fluency Program

Elfrieda H. Hiebert, Ph.D.

MODERN CURRICULUM PRESS

Pearson Learning Group

Program Reviewers and Consultants

Dr. Barbara A. Baird
Director of Federal Programs/Richardson ISD
Richardson, TX

Dr. Kate Kinsella
Dept. of Secondary Education and Step to College Program
San Francisco State University
San Francisco, CA

Pat Sears
Early Child Coordinator/Virginia Beach Public Schools
Virginia Beach, VA

Dr. Judith B. Smith
Supervisor of ESOL and World and Classical Languages/Baltimore City Public Schools
Baltimore, MD

The following people have contributed to the development of this product:

Art and Design: Adriano Farinella, Luis Ferreira, Dorothea Fox, Salita Mehta, Janice Noto-Helmers, Dan Thomas

Editorial: Lynn W. Kloss

Manufacturing: Michele Uhl

Marketing: Connie Buck

Production: Laura Benford-Sullivan, Jeffrey Engel

Publishing Operations: Jennifer Van Der Heide

Modern Curriculum Press
Pearson Learning Group

1-800-321-3106
www.pearsonlearning.com

Contents

Contents

SCIENCE **Sound**

Contents

Contents

Acknowledgments

All photographs © Pearson Learning unless otherwise noted.

Cover: Tony Stone Images/Chicago.

3: 3M Corporation. 4: Michael Newman/PhotoDisc, Inc. 5: Cameron Davidson/Stock Connection/PictureQuest. 6: Museo Archeologico, Florence, Italy/Art Resource. 7: Library of Congress. 8: Karl Bodmer/Wood River Gallery/PictureQuest. 12: 3M Corporation. 14: Herral Long. 16: Dupont & Company. 18: David Young Wolff/PhotoEdit/PictureQuest. 28: Amy Etra/PhotoEdit/PictureQuest. 30: Joseph Sohm/Corbis. 32: Michael Newman/PhotoDisc, Inc. 38: Cameron Davidson/Stock Connection/PictureQuest. 40: SuperStock, Inc. 42: Darryl Torckler/Stone. 44: Philip Rodrigues Singer. 46: Chris Shinn/Stone. 52: Stone/Getty Images. 54: Museo Archeologico, Florence, Italy/Art Resource, NY. 56: Charles & Josette Lenars/Corbis. 58: Sylvain Grandadam/Stone/Getty Images. 60: Brian Brake/Photo Researchers, Inc. 66: Library of Congress. 68, 70: Bettman/Corbis. 74: Bob Darmmirch/The Image Works. 80: Giraudon/Art Resource, NY. 82: Karl Bodmer/Wood River Gallery/PictureQuest. 86: Brown Brothers. 88: AP/Wide World Photos.

Inventions

Clint Lenz's glow-in-the-dark toilet seat
helped him find the toilet in the dark.

What Is an Invention?

An invention is a new thing or a new way of doing something. TVs, cars, bikes—all of these were invented[25] once. Sometimes inventions are made when people have a problem and someone looks for a way to solve the problem. Most inventions come about after[50] lots of hard work. Sometimes people invent one thing when they are trying to invent something else.

Clint Lenz was nine years old when he[75] invented the glow-in-the-dark toilet seat. He was tired of trying to find the toilet in the dark. So Clint Lenz solved the[100] problem by painting a toilet seat with glow-in-the-dark paint. That is how he became an inventor.[119]

Inventions

Arthur Fry found a new use for a weak glue.

Finding the Right Use

Sometimes people don't know that they have invented something useful. Spencer Silver made a new glue. The new glue made things[25] stick together. However, it was too weak to hold things together for long. Spencer Silver stopped working on the glue.

Arthur Fry knew about the[50] glue and found a good use for it. Arthur Fry always lost his place in the songbook at church. He put the weak glue on[75] little pieces of paper and stuck them on the pages of his songbook. Now, Arthur Fry could be at the right place in the songbook.[100] In addition, the weak glue didn't hurt the songbook. That's how the little notes you stick on papers and books were invented.[122]

Inventions

Rebecca Shroeder solved her problem
with glow-in-the-dark paint, too.

Solving a Problem

Rebecca Schroeder was ten years old when
she invented something that nurses now use in
hospitals. When Rebecca Schroeder did her
homework[25] in the car after dark, she couldn't see it.
Like Clint Lenz, Rebecca Schroeder solved her
problem with glow-in-the-dark paint. She covered[50]
a clipboard with the paint. Then she could see the
words on a paper that was on the clipboard.

Rebecca Schroeder used this idea to[75] invent
a sheet that could help people write in the dark.
At night, nurses in hospitals need to take notes
about sick people. If they[100] use Rebecca Schroeder's
glow-in-the-dark sheet on their clipboard, they
can write in the dark. Sick people can keep on
sleeping.[123]

Inventions

Stephanie Kwolek invented a material
that can save people's lives.

An Invention that Saves Lives

In 1964, Stephanie Kwolek was looking for a way to make car tires stronger. She tried many things. She tried[25] lots of different materials. However, none of them worked well. At last, she made something that was not like any material that anyone had ever[50] made before. This new material was five times stronger than steel. This material became known as Kevlar.

With Kevlar, car tires were stronger. Kevlar has[75] many other uses, too. Kevlar can save people's lives. It is used in safety helmets that people wear when they ride their bikes. When you[100] put on your safety helmet before you ride your bike, you can thank Stephanie Kwolek for helping to keep you safe.[121]

Inventions

Calculators are inventions that have gotten better over time.

An Invention that Keeps Changing

Some inventions keep changing. They get better. A calculator is one invention that is still changing. A calculator is like[25] an adding machine. People use calculators to add numbers and to do math problems. With a calculator, you can do math problems quickly.

The first[50] calculators were very big. They took up a whole room. It took many people to use the first calculators. They cost a lot of money.[75] Today, some calculators cost only a few dollars. They are small, too. New calculators can be smaller than your hand.

Today, children use calculators by[100] themselves. Calculators can do more kinds of math problems than they used to do. Like many inventions, calculators keep getting better.[121]

Write words that will help you remember what you learned.

What Is an Invention?

_____

_____

_____

_____

Finding the Right Use

_____

_____

_____

_____

Solving a Problem

_____

_____

_____

_____

An Invention that Saves Lives

_____

_____

_____

_____

An Invention that Keeps Changing

_____

_____

_____

_____

What Is an Invention?

1. What is an invention?

   Ⓐ a person who invents something

   Ⓑ a company that makes new things

   Ⓒ a new thing or new way of doing something

   Ⓓ a problem that needs to be solved

2. How are inventions made?

_____

_____

_____

Finding the Right Use

1. The main idea of "Finding the Right Use" is that _____

   Ⓐ every good invention is useful in some way.

   Ⓑ an invention can sometimes be used in an unexpected way.

   Ⓒ Arthur Fry invented a songbook.

   Ⓓ everyone can be an inventor.

2. How did Arthur Fry use Spencer Silver's glue?

_____

_____

_____

Solving a Problem

1. What did Rebecca Schroeder invent?

    Ⓐ glow-in-the-dark books

    Ⓑ a new way to do homework

    Ⓒ a glow-in-the-dark sheet for writing in the dark

    Ⓓ a clipboard for writing in the car

2. Retell what you learned in "Solving a Problem."

_____

_____

_____

An Invention that Saves Lives

1. The main idea of "An Invention that Saves Lives" is _____

    Ⓐ that some inventions make a big difference in people's lives.

    Ⓑ that some inventions can earn people a lot of money.

    Ⓒ that car tires are stronger now.

    Ⓓ that Stephanie Kwolek is a good inventor.

2. Retell how Stephanie Kwolek invented Kevlar.

_____

_____

_____

An Invention that Keeps Changing

1. "An Invention that Keeps Changing" is MAINLY about _____

Ⓐ how some inventions, such as calculators, get better.

Ⓑ how everyone uses calculators today.

Ⓒ how children use calculators.

Ⓓ how inventors can make any invention better.

2. What are three ways calculators have changed?

_____

_____

_____

Connect Your Ideas

1. What would you tell someone to do who wanted to invent something new?

_____

_____

_____

2. Describe something that you would like to invent.

_____

_____

_____

Simple Machines

Wedges, like this knife, can be used to cut things.

What Is a Simple Machine?

When you hear the word *machine*, you probably think of a car or a TV. However, some machines are simple.[25] You might not even think of them as machines. Once you know how simple machines work, you can see how other machines work.

Think about[50] someone cutting an apple with a knife. The cutting is easy because the knife is a wedge. A wedge is a simple machine that can[75] be used to cut or push apart something. An ax is another wedge. It can be used to chop down trees. You use wedges at[100] home and at school. Some people use wedges at work. Including the wedge, there are five kinds of simple machines.[120]

Simple Machines

Wheels and axles can be used in many ways.

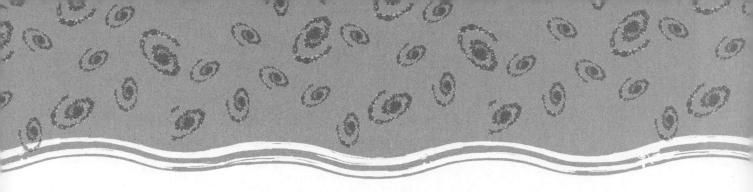

The Most Important Machine of All

Until one simple machine was invented, people could only travel by foot, in boats, or on animals like horses.[25] Wagons, trains, trucks, cars, and bikes all use the simple machine called the wheel and axle. There were no wagons, trucks, trains, cars, or bikes[50] until the wheel and axle was invented.

You have seen a wheel, but you might not have looked at one carefully. A wheel needs an[75] axle around which to turn. If you look at a wagon, you will see that the two rear wheels are joined by a bar. That[100] bar is the axle. The two front wheels are also joined by an axle. The wheel and axle makes many things move.[122]

Simple Machines

Inclined planes can help people travel.

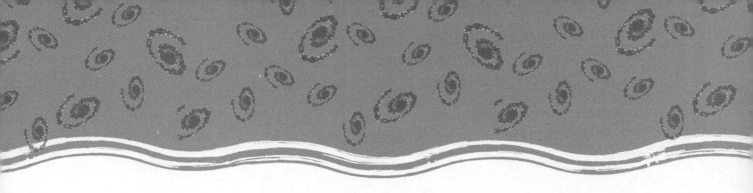

The Simplest Machine of All

You have seen ramps around buildings. Ramps make it easier for people in wheelchairs to travel around. A ramp is[25] the simplest machine of all. It is a kind of simple machine called an inclined plane. Inclined planes are flat and slanted.

A ramp makes[50] it easier to load heavy boxes onto trucks. With a ramp, you can push a heavy box into the truck. Without a ramp, you have[75] to lift the box into the truck.

Your chair is probably held together with screws. If you look closely at a screw, you will see[100] slanted ridges going up and around the screw. These ridges are curved, but they really are one long inclined plane.[120]

Pulleys help people move things.

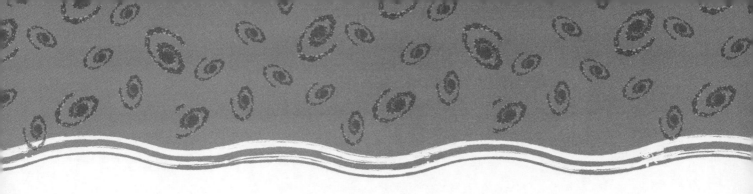

Pull Down, Lift Up

Have you ever wondered how a flag gets to the top of the pole outside your school? A simple machine called [25] a pulley makes it easy to get flags up and down high poles. A pulley is a wheel with a rope moving around it. When [50] someone pulls down on one end of the rope, something is lifted up on the other end. When you open the blinds on a window [75] by pulling on the cord, you're using a pulley.

Pulleys are good for lifting heavy loads, too. A crane that lifts huge blocks to the [100] top of a high building uses pulleys. A ski lift uses pulleys to take people to the tops of mountains. [120]

Simple Machines

A seesaw is a kind of simple machine.

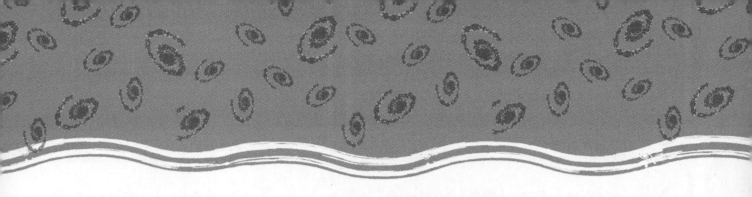

Playing on a Simple Machine

If you have ever been on a seesaw, you have played on a simple machine. This machine is called a[25] lever. On a seesaw, you and your friend sit across from one another. If you both weigh about the same amount, you will take turns[50] going up and down.

The seesaw has a board that sits on a resting place. This resting place is called a fulcrum. A fulcrum helps[75] you move or lift something. The fulcrum of a seesaw helps you pick up your friend.

Levers can also help you lift the lid of[100] a can or pick up a heavy box. As you can see, levers are simple machines that are very useful.[120]

Simple Machines

Write words that will help you remember what you learned.

What Is a Simple Machine?

_____

_____

_____

_____

The Most Important Machine of All

_____

_____

_____

_____

The Simplest Machine of All

_____

_____

_____

_____

Pull Down, Lift Up

_____

_____

_____

_____

Playing on a Simple Machine

_____

_____

_____

_____

What Is a Simple Machine?

1. Which is an example of a simple machine?

  Ⓐ an apple

  Ⓑ a knife

  Ⓒ a car

  Ⓓ an airplane

2. How do wedges work?

_____

_____

_____

The Most Important Machine of All

1. Another good name for "The Most Important Machine of All" is _____

  Ⓐ "Simple Machines."

  Ⓑ "The Wheel and Axle."

  Ⓒ "How a Wedge Works."

  Ⓓ "Why Axles Move."

2. How does the wheel and axle work?

_____

_____

_____

The Simplest Machine of All

1. The main idea of "The Simplest Machine of All" is _____

   Ⓐ that ramps are the simplest machines of all.

   Ⓑ that ramps move easily.

   Ⓒ that screws are the simplest machines of all.

   Ⓓ that ramps are flat and slanted.

2. Retell what you learned in "The Simplest Machine of All."

   _____

   _____

   _____

Pull Down, Lift Up

1. What is a pulley?

   Ⓐ a wheel with a rope moving around it

   Ⓑ a rope attached to a flag

   Ⓒ a wheel with a ramp moving around it

   Ⓓ a wheel, an axle, and a rope

2. How does a pulley work?

   _____

   _____

   _____

Playing on a Simple Machine

1. "Playing on a Simple Machine" is MAINLY about ____

   Ⓐ how simple machines work.

   Ⓑ how seesaws work with pulleys and levers.

   Ⓒ how a lever works.

   Ⓓ simple machines people use for work.

2. Explain how a lever works.

   _____

   _____

   _____

Connect Your Ideas

1. Describe two simple machines that you see around you.

   _____

   _____

   _____

2. Give two different ways people use one simple machine you have read about.

   _____

   _____

   _____

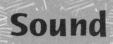

Sound

A barking dog makes sound waves.

What Is Sound?

A dog barks. A bell rings. A book falls to the floor. When these things happen, you hear sounds. Movements cause sound waves to form. Then these sound waves travel through the air. A book that falls from a desk to the floor makes more movement in the air than a paper does. This is because the book is heavier than the paper. The book makes a loud noise when it hits the floor. The paper makes a soft noise.

Sound waves are too small to see. Yet the eardrums inside your ears feel the sound waves. When the sound waves hit the eardrums inside your ears, your eardrums feel the sound waves. That is how you hear sound.

Sound moves faster through water than through air.

The Speed of Sound

Did you hear a sound? Something moved
and made sound waves. Those sound waves moved
through the air at the speed[25] of about 1,000 feet
per second to get to your eardrums. This speed
may seem fast, but it is not as fast as the speed[50]
of light. Sound moves more slowly than light.
This means that you see things far away before
you hear them. That's why you see a[75] plane
before you hear it.

Sound waves can move at different speeds.
Sound waves move more quickly on hot days than
on cold days. They[100] also move more quickly through
water than through air. The next time you go
swimming, listen to how sounds move under water.[122]

Sound

Echoes in caves are caused by bouncing sound waves.

Hearing It Two Times

Make a noise in a room that has lots of rugs. You may not hear yourself. Soft materials like rugs soak[25] up sound waves. Now make a noise in an empty room. You will probably hear yourself very clearly. This is because sound waves bounce off[50] the walls of an empty room.

Sometimes sounds happen more than once. These bouncing sound waves are called an echo. You will probably hear an[75] echo if you make a sound near mountains or in a cave. The hard rocks do not soak up the sound waves. Instead, the sound[100] waves bounce back. You may even hear more than one echo. What you say may bounce back many times.[119]

Sound

The sound effects used in movies can be made with everyday things.

Sound Effects

When you watch a movie, you often hear sounds like thunder or a crash. The thunder and crash sounds in movies are called[25] sound effects. Today, people can use computers to make sound effects. Computers copy the sounds you hear when there is thunder or a crash. Before[50] computers, everyday things were used to make sound effects.

You can use everyday things to make sound effects, too. Fill a box with small rocks.[75] Shut your eyes and slowly move the box up and down. Can you hear an army marching? Next, pour seeds onto a metal tray. Ask[100] your friends to shut their eyes. When they hear the seeds hitting the metal tray, your friends will think it is raining.[122]

Sound

Jet planes make very loud sounds that can hurt people's ears.

Can Sounds Hurt?

Sounds can hurt people's ears. However, a sound has to be very loud to hurt someone's ears. The loudness or the softness[25] of sounds is measured in decibels. When you talk softly to a friend, the sound measures about 20 decibels.

Sounds of 120 decibels or more[50] hurt people's ears. A very loud sound that measures 140 decibels is the sound that a jet plane makes when it takes off. People have[75] to be right next to the plane when it takes off for their ears to be hurt. People who work near jets put plugs in[100] their ears when the planes take off. The ear plugs or covers stop some of the sound from getting inside their ears.[122]

 **Sound**

Write words that will help you remember what you learned.

What Is Sound?

① move met cause sound som
② sound travel trough air
③ when sound hit
  eardrum in ear
  you hear sounds

The Speed of Sound

① Sound wave speed
  6000 feet per second
② sound moves different
  speed ③ sound move
  quickly on hot day than
  cold day.

Hearing It Two Times

Sound Effects

Can Sounds Hurt?

What Is Sound?

1. Another good name for "What Is Sound?" is _____

   Ⓐ "The Sounds Things Make."

   Ⓑ "Dogs Make Sounds."

   Ⓒ "How Things Make Sounds."

   Ⓓ "Sounds Are Noises We Hear Around Us."

2. How are sounds made?

this is how you hear sounds. first a move ment happnes, then it travles throughthe air. After It travles it his your ear drum, Thats how it happnes.

The Speed of Sound

1. The main idea of "The Speed of Sound" is _____

   Ⓐ how quickly light waves move.

   Ⓑ how quickly sound waves move.

   Ⓒ why we hear sounds.

   Ⓓ how sound moves through water.

2. Retell what you learned in "The Speed of Sound."

I learned that the speed of sound moves quicheron hot day and slower in cold days

More.

Hearing It Two Times

1. Another good name for "Hearing It Two Times" is _____

    Ⓐ "Sounds in Caves."

    Ⓑ "Soaking up Sound."

    Ⓒ "Bouncing Sound Waves."

    Ⓓ "Hearing Yourself."

2. What is an echo?

_____

_____

_____

Sound Effects

1. "Sound Effects" is MAINLY about _____

    Ⓐ the people who make sound effects.

    Ⓑ how computers make sound effects.

    Ⓒ how sound effects are made.

    Ⓓ the kinds of sounds that rocks can make.

2. What are sound effects?

_____

_____

_____

Can Sounds Hurt?

1. You could read "Can Sounds Hurt?" to learn about _____

    Ⓐ if sounds can hurt people.

    Ⓑ how people and animals make sounds.

    Ⓒ how sounds can be stopped.

    Ⓓ if all sounds can hurt people.

2. How can people keep their ears from being hurt by sounds?

_____

_____

_____

Connect Your Ideas

1. What are two things you learned about sound?

_____

_____

_____

2. Suppose there was another reading in this unit. Would you expect it to be about drawing or about music? Why?

_____

_____

_____

Ancient Egypt

The Nile River runs through Egypt.

Egypt in Ancient Times

The Nile River runs through the country of Egypt. Until about 200 years ago, the Nile River flooded every year. This[25] flooding happened for thousands of years. The floods left soil on the land for six miles on each side of the river. This soil was[50] good for growing crops.

The river also helped the people of Egypt travel from one place to another. People could buy and sell things easily[75] by moving them on the river. The good crops and the easy travel helped make Egypt a rich country.

There is still a country called[100] Egypt. When we talk about the things that happened in Egypt thousands of years ago, we call it ancient Egypt.[120]

Ancient Egypt

eat   fish   bird

People in ancient Egypt wrote with hieroglyphics.
The drawings at the top of the picture are hieroglyphics.

Writing in Ancient Egypt

All of the words in English use the same 26 letters. These 26 letters make up the English alphabet. The letters[25] in the alphabet help us sound words out. How would you write if there were no alphabet?

Before people used an alphabet, they wrote with[50] pictures and signs. The pictures and signs used in ancient Egypt are called hieroglyphics. Every word had its own picture or sign. So people had[75] to go to school for many years to learn to write with hieroglyphics.

People in Egypt no longer use hieroglyphics. As we do in English,[100] people in Egypt today use an alphabet when they write. Alphabets allow people to make many words out of a few letters.[122]

Kings and queens in ancient Egypt were made into mummies after they died.

Mummies

You may have seen living mummies in movies. Real mummies are not alive like they are in the movies. When kings and queens died[25] in ancient Egypt, people made their bodies into mummies.

First, the brain, liver, and lungs were taken out. The brain, liver, and lungs were put[50] into stone jars. The heart was usually left inside the body. Special plants were put on the body. Then the body was wrapped with long[75] strips of cloth. A frame was put around the body. The frame was painted with pictures.

In modern times, people found some mummies and took[100] off the strips of cloth. The mummies looked very much like the bodies had looked right after the people died.[120]

Ancient Egypt

This is a pyramid in Egypt. The sides of
pyramids meet in a point at the top.

The Pyramids

The mummies of the kings and queens were kept in special buildings. These buildings are called pyramids. A pyramid has four slanting sides[25] that meet in a point at the top. The biggest pyramid is called the Great Pyramid.

There are more than two million stone blocks in[50] the Great Pyramid. To get an idea of the size of the Great Pyramid, picture a refrigerator. Each one of the two million stone blocks[75] in the Great Pyramid is as heavy as 25 refrigerators.

The workers had to put these heavy stone blocks in just the right place. If[100] they did not get a stone block in the right place, the four slanting sides would not meet at the top.[121]

This necklace was worn by someone in ancient Egypt.

Looking Good in Ancient Egypt

In ancient Egypt, men and women wore make-up. People put red paint on their cheeks and lips. They wore [25] green paint around their eyes. This green paint was not used only to make them look pretty. The paint also helped the people to keep [50] their eyes safe from the bright sun.

Even children wore jewelry in ancient Egypt. Kings and queens wore jewelry made of gold. Gold jewelry showed [75] that people were rich.

Men, women, and children liked to wear necklaces most. Necklaces were often made from stones, glass, and clay. The stones, glass, [100] and clay could make a necklace very heavy. It must have been hard to play in a heavy necklace. [119]

Ancient Egypt

Write words that will help you remember what you learned.

Egypt in Ancient Times

_____

_____

_____

_____

Writing in Ancient Egypt

_____

_____

_____

_____

Mummies

_____

_____

_____

_____

The Pyramids

_____

_____

_____

_____

Looking Good in Ancient Egypt

_____

_____

_____

_____

Egypt in Ancient Times

1. Another good name for "Egypt in Ancient Times" is _____

 Ⓐ "Flooding in Egypt."

 Ⓑ "Egypt and the Nile River."

 Ⓒ "Egypt Today."

 Ⓓ "Traveling in Egypt."

2. What was ancient Egypt like?

_____

_____

_____

Writing in Ancient Egypt

1. The main idea of "Writing in Ancient Egypt" is _____

 Ⓐ people in Egypt today use hieroglyphics.

 Ⓑ people in ancient Egypt wrote using signs and pictures.

 Ⓒ signs and pictures make up an alphabet.

 Ⓓ people in ancient Egypt created the first alphabet.

2. How did people write in ancient Egypt?

_____

_____

_____

Mummies

1. Why did the ancient Egyptians make mummies?

ⓐ to save the bodies of everyone

ⓑ to keep people alive

ⓒ to make art

ⓓ to save the bodies of kings and queens

2. What were the steps of making a mummy in ancient Egypt?

_____

_____

_____

The Pyramids

1. "The Pyramids" is MAINLY about _____

ⓐ how the Great Pyramid looks and how it was built.

ⓑ how kings and queens were buried.

ⓒ how to visit the Great Pyramid today.

ⓓ how long the Great Pyramid has lasted.

2. Describe the Great Pyramid.

_____

_____

_____

Looking Good in Ancient Egypt

1. What is the most important idea in "Looking Good in Ancient Egypt"?

   Ⓐ Make-up was used to protect Egyptians from the sun.

   Ⓑ Both men and women wore make-up in ancient Egypt.

   Ⓒ Ancient Egyptians wore make-up and jewelry.

   Ⓓ Children wore jewelry in ancient Egypt.

2. What might a person from ancient Egypt wear to look good?

   _____

   _____

   _____

Connect Your Ideas

1. How was life in ancient Egypt different from your life today?

   _____

   _____

   _____

2. Suppose there was another reading in this unit. Would you expect it to be about modern Egypt? Why or why not?

   _____

   _____

   _____

People wrote with feather pens in 1776.

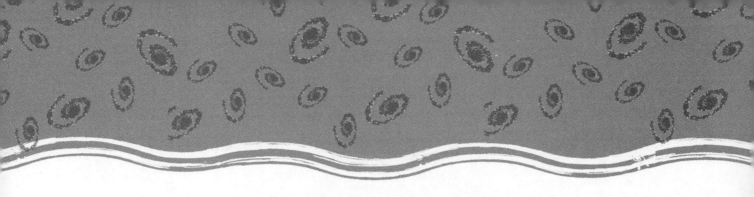

Changes in How We Communicate

Today, we can share news by calling friends on the telephone or writing to them on the computer. The ways[25] in which people communicate messages have changed a lot since our country began in 1776.

In 1776, there was only one way to communicate with[50] friends who lived far away. People needed to write their message on paper. They often used a feather pen. They dipped the hard point of[75] the feather into a pot of ink to write a word or two. Then the feather needed to be dipped into the ink again.

Mail[100] was sent by horseback. It could take weeks or even months for someone to get a message. Messages move more quickly today.[122]

People often wrote letters with fountain pens in 1910.

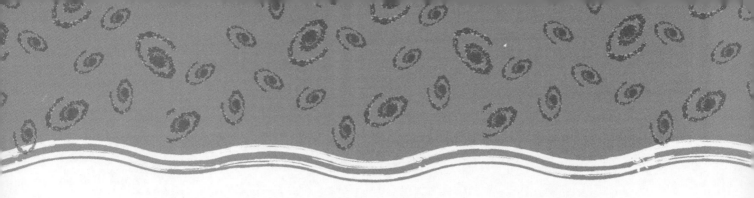

Your Great-grandparents: 1910

In 1910, your great-grandparents may have been in third grade. If they wanted to communicate with friends who lived far[25] away, they wrote a letter with a fountain pen. Fountain pens needed to be filled with ink. However, people could write a whole letter before[50] they needed to refill their fountain pen. Mail was sent by train, not by horses. Trains were faster than horses. Yet mail could still take[75] days or even weeks to arrive.

Telephones had been invented by 1910. Even so, most people did not often use the telephone. A telephone call[100] cost a lot of money. People also shared telephone lines with their neighbors. The neighbors could listen to each other's calls.[121]

The Ways We Communicate

Some people used a telephone to communicate with others in 1940.

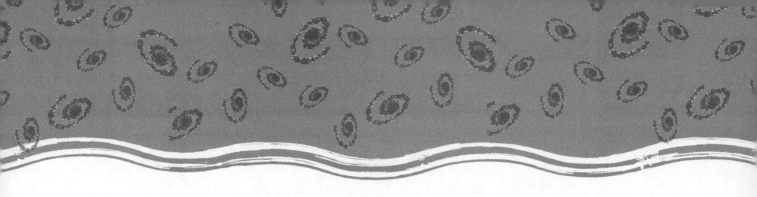

Your Grandparents: 1940

In 1940, your grandparents may have been in third grade. Many ways to communicate had been invented by then. Most third graders[25] still wrote their messages in letters, but they had ballpoint pens like those you use today. Letters arrived in just a few days because mail[50] was sent on trains, trucks, and even airplanes.

Your grandparents probably had a telephone in their home. Yet telephone calls still cost a lot of[75] money. In addition, telephone lines were still shared with others.

Your grandparents got their news from the radio in 1940. They didn't have TVs. However,[100] radios were as big as TVs are today. Families would sit by the radio and listen to many different kinds of shows.[122]

People received news quickly in 1970 by watching TV.

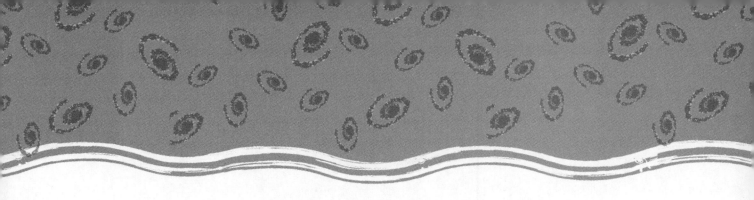

Your Parents: 1970

In 1970, your parents may have been in third grade. At that time, there were lots of ways for them to communicate[25] messages to one another. If they wrote letters to friends far away, the letters traveled quickly on jet airplanes. Telephone calls were cheaper. In addition,[50] many people had TVs, so news from around the world was communicated quickly. TVs also now had shows in color.

Today, people have a new[75] way to communicate with each other. They can use computers. Third graders in 1970 would not have used computers to do their homework or play[100] games. There were computers, but desktop computers had not yet been invented. In 1970, third-grade classrooms did not have computers.[121]

The Ways We Communicate

Today, computers help people send
and receive messages quickly.

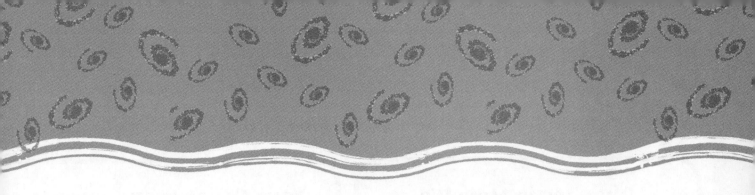

Communication Today

Today, people in the United States can communicate with one another in many ways. They can call friends on a cell phone. They[25] can type a message on a computer and send it. In seconds, the message can be read by someone who lives many miles away.

Video[50] machines can record pictures and voices to communicate messages. People can even send videos of messages by computer. Friends thousands of miles away can see[75] and hear the message quickly. From computers and TVs, people get news from around the world almost the second it happens.

Yet sometimes, it's still[100] fun to communicate messages the way that our great-grandparents did. All you need is paper, a pen, and a stamp.[121]

The Ways We Communicate

Write words that will help you remember what you learned.

Changes in How We Communicate

_____

_____

_____

Your Great-grandparents: 1910

_____

_____

_____

Your Grandparents: 1940

_____

_____

_____

Your Parents: 1970

_____

_____

_____

Communication Today

_____

_____

_____

_____

Changes in How We Communicate

1. How would someone send a message in 1776?

Ⓐ by calling the person on the telephone

Ⓑ by sending a message by stagecoach

Ⓒ by writing a letter and sending it by horseback

Ⓓ by having someone who is traveling tell the message

2. How did people communicate in 1776?

_____

_____

_____

Your Great-grandparents: 1910

1. Another good title for "Your Great-grandparents: 1910" is _____

Ⓐ "Communicating in 1910."

Ⓑ "Mail by Train."

Ⓒ "Telephones Changed Communication."

Ⓓ "How Mail was Delivered in 1910."

2. How did people send news in 1910?

_____

_____

_____

The Ways We Communicate

Your Grandparents: 1940

1. "Your Grandparents: 1940" is MAINLY about ——

   Ⓐ getting news by radio.

   Ⓑ faster mail service.

   Ⓒ the ways people communicated in 1940.

   Ⓓ how TV changed the world.

2. Write three ways that people learned about the news in 1940.

_____

_____

_____

Your Parents: 1970

1. What were the ways people communicated in 1970?

   Ⓐ by letter, telephone, and TV

   Ⓑ by letter, radio, and computer

   Ⓒ by computer and TV

   Ⓓ by radio and airplane

2. How did people communicate differently in 1970 from the way they communicate today?

_____

_____

_____

Communication Today

1. The main idea of "Communication Today" is _____

Ⓐ that computers have made communicating faster.

Ⓑ that people today have many ways to communicate.

Ⓒ that the best way to communicate is still by letter.

Ⓓ that people have more friends now.

2. How do people communicate today?

_____

_____

_____

Connect Your Ideas

1. What is the biggest change between communication in 1776 and today?

_____

_____

_____

2. Why do you think people still like to write letters today?

_____

_____

_____

Native Americans

Some Native Americans lived in towns like this
one when the European explorers came.

The First Americans

People have been living in North America for a long time. When explorers came to North America from Europe 500 years ago,[25] they were looking for a way to get to the Indies. Their maps did not show North America. The explorers traveled for a long time[50] on ships. When the explorers got to land, they thought they were in the Indies.

The European explorers found people when they landed in North[75] America. The explorers called these people Indians because they thought they had come to the Indies. Later, the explorers found out that they had come[100] to a new place. Europeans then called this new place America. The people who lived here first are now called Native Americans.[122]

Native Americans

Native Americans on the Great Plains lived in tents.

Native American Homes

When the European explorers first came to North America, there were about 300 groups of Native Americans. These groups were different from [25] one another.

In the east, Native Americans hunted and grew crops. They made houses of wood and bark. They lived in houses because they stayed [50] in one place to grow crops.

On the Great Plains, Native Americans hunted buffalo. They lived in tents that could be moved quickly. They needed [75] to follow the buffalo.

In the dry land of the southwest, Native Americans grew crops that did not need much water. They made houses out [100] of clay, sand, and straw.

In the northwest, Native Americans fished and cut down trees to make houses and boats. [120]

The girl is using sign language to say
"proud." The boy is saying "good."

Sign Language

You speak English. You may speak another language, too. What might you do if no one around you understood you?

Because they lived[25] far apart, Native American groups spoke different languages. When groups met, they could not understand one another. The Native Americans who lived on the Great[50] Plains made up a sign language. The sign language helped groups understand each other. You and your friends can try these signs, too.

To say[75] "hello," hold your hand up with the palm out. Move your hand in a circle. To say "home," put the tips of your fingers together[100] and against your chest. To say "thank you," keep the palms of both hands down. Now move your hands down low.[121]

Native Americans

Native American children played games like hockey.

Native Americans' Games

Hundreds of years ago, Native American children played games very much like the hockey and football that people play today. Like the[25] games of hockey and football of today, Native American children played their games with sticks and balls. They used sticks from branches of trees to[50] hit the balls. They made balls of wood, stone, animal skins, and bark from trees.

Native American children also played some games that most children[75] do not play today. In one of these games, they tossed or hit balls from one boat to another. Native American children had to be[100] careful when they played games like this in boats. If they were not careful, they would fall into the water.[120]

Native Americans

Today, there are many Native Americans in the government, like Senator Ben Nighthorse Campbell.

Native Americans Today

The lives of Native Americans changed after the explorers came to America. Their lands were soon gone. Many Native Americans died in wars and from illnesses. By 1900, many groups were very small. Laws kept Native Americans from having the same rights as other Americans.

Native Americans today can go to school, live, and work where they wish. They have the same rights as other Americans. The number of Native Americans has grown. Today, there are more than four times as many Native Americans as there were in 1900.

Native Americans are also working hard to keep alive the stories and ways of their groups. These stories and ways are an important part of what makes America special.

Native Americans

Write words that will help you remember what you learned.

The First Americans

_____

_____

_____

_____

Native American Homes

_____

_____

_____

_____

Sign Language

_____

_____

_____

_____

Native Americans' Games

_____

_____

_____

_____

Native Americans Today

_____

_____

_____

_____

The First Americans

1. Another good name for "The First Americans" is _____

Ⓐ "Finding the Indies."

Ⓑ "Explorers in North America."

Ⓒ "Maps of North America."

Ⓓ "How Native Americans Came to North America."

2. Why did the European explorers think they were in the Indies?

_____

_____

_____

Native American Homes

1. "Native American Homes" is MAINLY about _____

Ⓐ how Native American groups are like each other.

Ⓑ how Native Americans live today.

Ⓒ Native Americans in the Eastern United States.

Ⓓ how Native American groups are different from each another.

2. Describe two kinds of Native American homes.

_____

_____

_____

Native Americans

Sign Language

1. Why did Native Americans create sign language?

   Ⓐ to talk to each other over long distances

   Ⓑ to talk to Europeans

   Ⓒ to help different groups understand each other

   Ⓓ to help Europeans understand them

2. Retell what you learned about Native American sign language.

_____

_____

_____

Native Americans' Games

1. Native American children once played games that are like _____

   Ⓐ hockey and football of today.

   Ⓑ hockey and jump-rope of today.

   Ⓒ football and baseball of today.

   Ⓓ football and running games of today.

2. Describe a Native American game that children do not play today.

_____

_____

_____

Native Americans Today

1. How did the lives of Native Americans change after the explorers came?

    Ⓐ Many died in wars or from illness.

    Ⓑ Many moved to new homes in America.

    Ⓒ Many began to speak new languages.

    Ⓓ Many traveled to new places with the explorers.

2. How do Native Americans live today?

    _____

    _____

Connect Your Ideas

1. Suppose you were a Native American child living 500 years ago. What would a day in your life be like?

    _____

    _____

    _____

2. What do you think is the biggest change in the way Native Americans lived 500 years ago and today?

    _____

    _____

    _____

Reading Log • Level C • Book 3

	I Read This	New Words I Learned	New Facts I Learned	What Else I Want to Learn About This Subject
Inventions				
What Is an Invention?				
Finding the Right Use				
Solving a Problem				
An Invention that Saves Lives				
An Invention that Keeps Changing				
Simple Machines				
What Is a Simple Machine?				
The Most Important Machine of All				
The Simplest Machine of All				
Pull Down, Lift Up				
Playing on a Simple Machine				
Sound				
What Is Sound?				
The Speed of Sound				
Hearing It Two Times				
Sound Effects				
Can Sounds Hurt?				

	I Read This	New Words I Learned	New Facts I Learned	What Else I Want to Learn About This Subject
Ancient Egypt				
Egypt in Ancient Times				
Writing in Ancient Egypt				
Mummies				
The Pyramids				
Looking Good in Ancient Egypt				
The Ways We Communicate				
Changes in How We Communicate				
Your Great-grandparents: 1910				
Your Grandparents: 1940				
Your Parents: 1970				
Communication Today				
Native Americans				
The First Americans				
Native American Homes				
Sign Language				
Native Americans' Games				
Native Americans Today				

Self-Check Graph

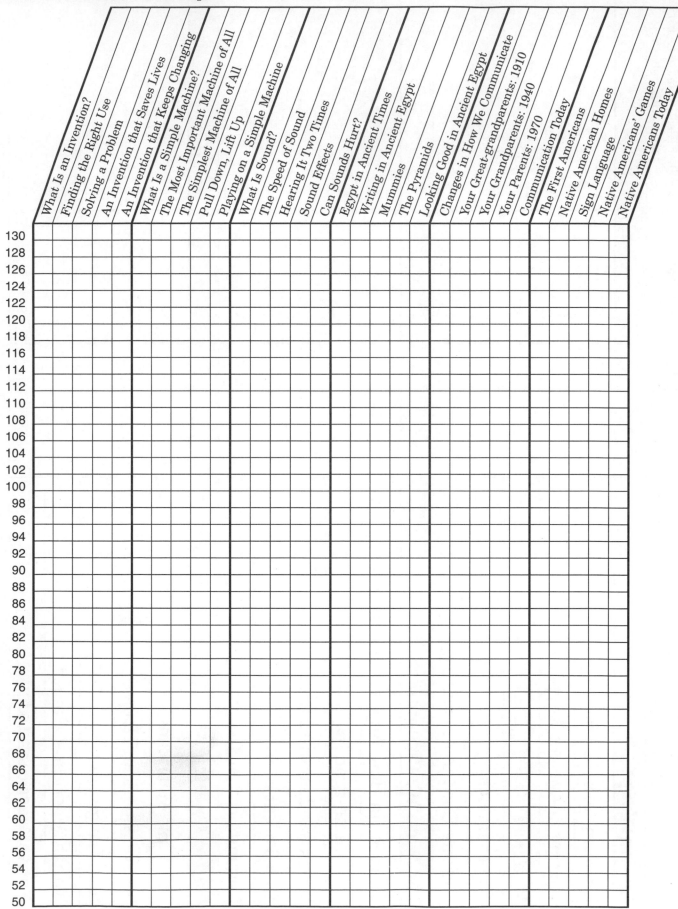

Column headers (left to right):
What Is an Invention? · Finding the Right Use · Solving a Problem · An Invention that Saves Lives · An Invention that Keeps Changing · What Is a Simple Machine? · The Most Important Machine of All · The Simplest Machine of All · Pull Down, Lift Up · Playing on a Simple Machine · What Is Sound? · The Speed of Sound · Hearing It Two Times · Sound Effects · Can Sounds Hurt? · Egypt in Ancient Times · Writing in Ancient Egypt · Mummies · The Pyramids · Looking Good in Ancient Egypt · Changes in How We Communicate · Your Great-grandparents: 1910 · Your Grandparents: 1940 · Your Parents: 1970 · Communication Today · The First Americans · Native American Homes · Sign Language · Native Americans' Games · Native Americans Today

Row labels (top to bottom): 130, 128, 126, 124, 122, 120, 118, 116, 114, 112, 110, 108, 106, 104, 102, 100, 98, 96, 94, 92, 90, 88, 86, 84, 82, 80, 78, 76, 74, 72, 70, 68, 66, 64, 62, 60, 58, 56, 54, 52, 50